Where Is Antarctica?

by Sarah Fabiny

illustrated by Jerry Hoare

Penguin Workshop
An Imprint of Penguin Random House

For every young adventurer who
wants to go see the world—SF

PENGUIN WORKSHOP
Penguin Young Readers Group
An Imprint of Penguin Random House LLC

Copyright © 2019 by Penguin Random House LLC. All rights reserved. Published by Penguin Workshop, an imprint of Penguin Random House LLC, 345 Hudson Street, New York, New York 10014. PENGUIN and PENGUIN WORKSHOP are trademarks of Penguin Books Ltd. WHO HQ & Design is a registered trademark of Penguin Random House LLC. Printed in the USA.

Library of Congress Cataloging-in-Publication Data is available.

ISBN 9781524787592 (paperback)   10 9 8 7 6 5 4 3 2 1
ISBN 9781524787608 (library binding)   10 9 8 7 6 5 4 3 2 1

Contents

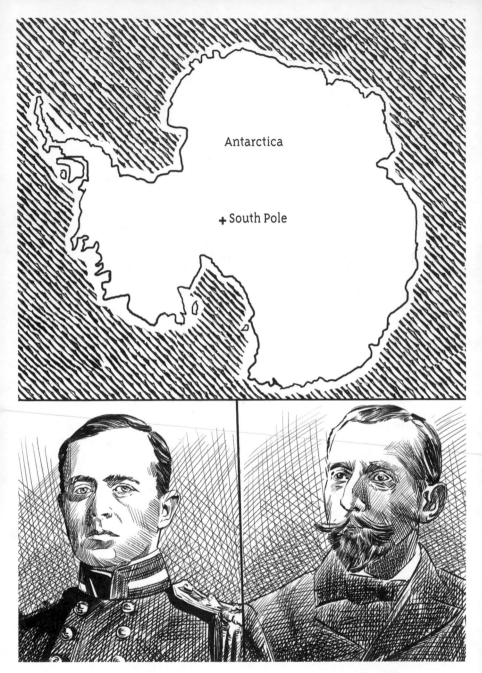

Robert Falcon Scott   Roald Amundsen

Where Is Antarctica?

In 1910, Roald Amundsen, an explorer from Norway, and Robert Falcon Scott, a British naval officer, were in a battle. They each wanted to be the first person to reach the South Pole on the continent of Antarctica. Both were great explorers and adventurers. Both had already made several daring expeditions in their lives.

Amundsen had been among the first group of men to spend a winter in Antarctica. He was also part of a crew that sailed through the Northwest Passage in northern Canada.

Scott had joined the British navy when he was just thirteen years old. In 1901, when he was thirty-three years old, he led the first expedition to the South Pole. He and his team did not make it, but Scott was determined to keep trying.

In the summer of 1910, both Amundsen and Scott set off on separate journeys to reach the South Pole. Each was determined to beat the other. Even reaching the coast of Antarctica was going to be difficult. Once each man and his crew landed, they still had to cross almost eight hundred miles of treacherous snow and ice.

In September 1911, Amundsen and his men started trekking from the coast to the South Pole.

Dogs pulled their sleds. Scott and his men began the hike in November 1911. They had brought ponies as well as sled dogs to help them make the journey. Both parties encountered severe temperatures and raging blizzards. But neither party was willing to give up and turn back.

In this race to the pole, who—if anybody—would get there first and make history?

CHAPTER 1
At the Bottom of the World

Did you know that the ground underneath your feet is always moving? The outer layer of Earth's crust is made up of large areas called tectonic plates. They are separated from each other and they are always shifting, but at a very, very slow pace. As the plates move, they come together, drift apart, or slide past each other.

The movement of the plates has been occurring for millions of years and accounts for why Earth's seven continents are where they are configured now. Three hundred million years ago, however, all the continents were joined together. They formed a supercontinent called Pangaea (say: pan-JEE-uh). An ocean called Panthalassa (say: PAN-thuh-LASS-uh) surrounded Pangaea. Many scientists believe that the interior area of Pangaea was a huge desert.

Around 200 million years ago, during the Triassic period, Pangaea began to break up as the plates moved apart. Two landmasses, called Laurasia (say: lor-AY-zhuh) and Gondwana (say: gon-DWAH-nuh), were formed. Laurasia was made up of what are now North America, Europe, and Asia. Gondwana was made up of what are now Africa, South America, Australia, India, and Antarctica.

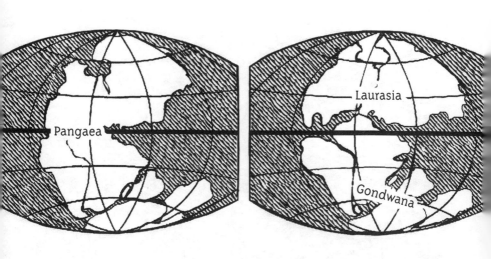

During this time, Earth's climate was much warmer than it is now. There was no ice on Antarctica, and plants and animals thrived there.

About 100 million years ago, during the Cretaceous period, Laurasia and Gondwana started breaking apart, and around 85 million years ago, Antarctica and Australia began to split apart.

Ankylosaurs (armored dinosaurs) made their way through forests of conifer trees and ferns, and plesiosaurs swam in the surrounding oceans.

Earth's plates continued to move and change the appearance of the planet's surface. By about 30 million years ago, Antarctica and Australia had completely separated.

After that, Antarctica drifted to the south and Australia drifted northward. During this time, Earth's climate began to cool, and Antarctica

started to freeze over. The tectonic plates continued to move and the continents drifted to their current positions. Antarctica ended up at the bottom of the world. And ice has covered it for several million years. A place that had once been warm and was home to many plants and animals became frigid and frozen.

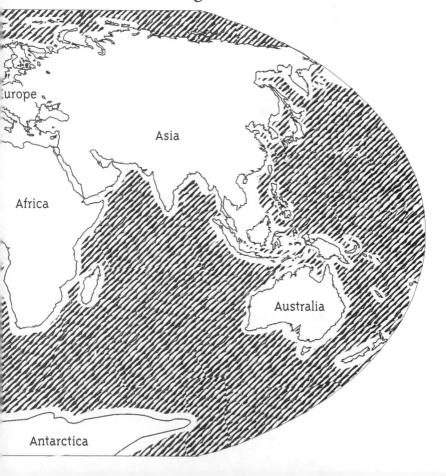

Continental Drift

If you look at a map of the world, you see that the east coast of South America and the west coast of Africa look like two pieces of a jigsaw puzzle that fit together. Scientists had noticed this once fairly accurate

Frank B. Taylor

maps of the entire Earth were created. But they could not explain how the two continents would have been connected and then split apart.

An American geologist named Frank B. Taylor first proposed the theory of "continental drift" in 1908. But the paper he wrote about his theory was ignored and forgotten.

Over the next several decades, because of new scientific equipment, scientists were able to study the ocean floor. They saw that there were cracks in the seabed that could be edges of the sections that make up Earth's surface. So Taylor had been right. By the mid-1960s, the theory of continental drift, or plate tectonics as it came to be known, was recognized as one of the most important theories about the formation of Earth's surface.

CHAPTER 2
Mountains, Volcanoes, and Lots of Ice

Of the seven continents on our planet, Antarctica is the third smallest in terms of size (Australia is smallest, then Europe). And its nearest neighbor, South America, is about six hundred miles away. The Southern Ocean surrounds Antarctica on all sides. The harsh climate has meant that no civilization ever developed there. No ancient people ever landed on Antarctica and decided it would be a good place to live!

About 90 percent of the world's ice is found on Antarctica. Some of the tallest mountains on the planet are there. However, you can't see them because they are covered by ice. The ice is so heavy that it has pushed these areas of land far below sea level. The weight also causes the ice to spread out toward the coasts. The ice covers valleys, lakes, and even volcanoes. The ice that covers these landforms averages one and a half miles in thickness. That's about the same as stacking twenty-six Statues of Liberty on top of each other.

This cold, icy continent is divided into two parts by the two-thousand-mile-long Transantarctic Mountains. That makes this mountain range longer than the Himalayas in Asia. The highest peak in the mountain range is Mount Kirkpatrick. It rises to 14,856 feet, which is taller than any of the peaks in the Rocky Mountains.

Mighty Mountains

Along the border of Nepal, Tibet, and India runs the Himalaya mountain range, home to the tallest peaks on our planet. It includes Mount Everest, whose peak rises just over 29,000 feet into the sky. The Andes Mountains run along the entire western edge of South America. The highest peak there is Mount Aconcagua, which is 22,837 feet tall. Mount Denali in Alaska is the tallest mountain in North America. It is 20,310 feet tall. The Rocky Mountains stretch from Canada to New Mexico. This mountain range includes more than twenty-five peaks over 14,000 feet tall.

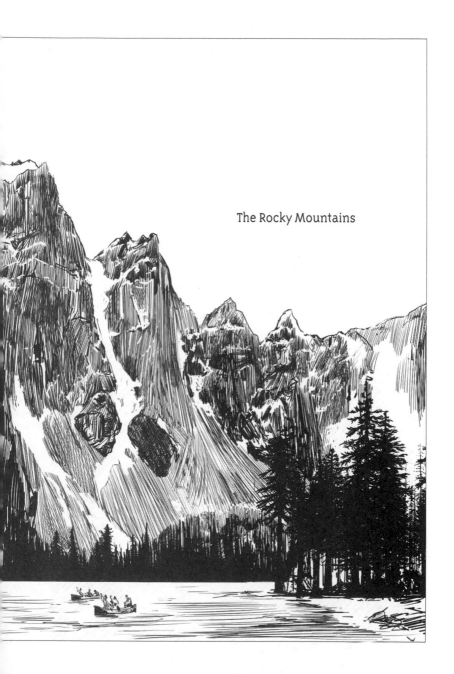

The Rocky Mountains

The Transantarctic Mountains split Antarctica into East Antarctica, sometimes called "Greater Antarctica," and West Antarctica, or "Lesser Antarctica." East Antarctica makes up about two-thirds of the continent. It also contains the geographic South Pole, which is the southernmost point on Earth. Few people have traveled to this area because the deep cracks in the thick ice make it very difficult to cross. This part of Antarctica is the most isolated place on the planet.

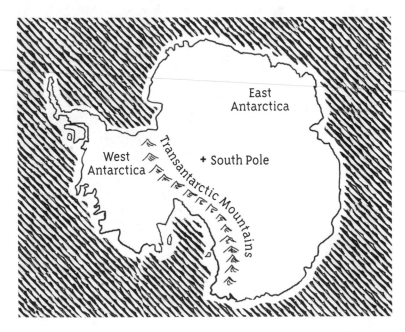

Lambert Glacier

East Antarctica has several glaciers. A glacier is a large, slow-moving area of thick ice that remains frozen from one year to the next. It flows slowly over the land underneath it. The largest glacier in the world, the Lambert Glacier, is in East Antarctica.

Long and Thin versus Small and Round

When you look at Antarctica on a map, it looks like a long strip of land that stretches from one edge of the world to the other. But this depiction of Antarctica is misleading. The better way to

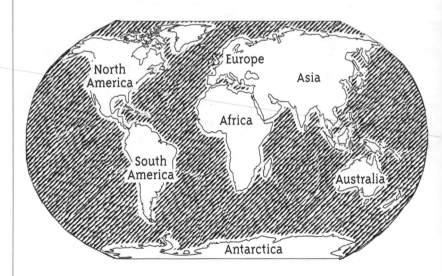

understand the shape, size, and position of Antarctica is by looking at a globe. Rather than being long and thin, this continent at the bottom of the world is quite round in shape.

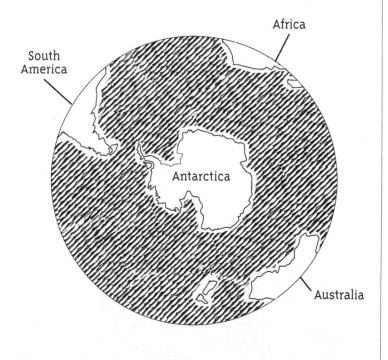

East Antarctica is also home to Lake Vostok. Although it is one of the world's largest lakes, it wasn't discovered until the 1960s. That is because you cannot see it on the surface of the land. It lies below two miles of ice. Even though it is buried under the ice, scientists have discovered tiny organisms, including many types of bacteria, living in it.

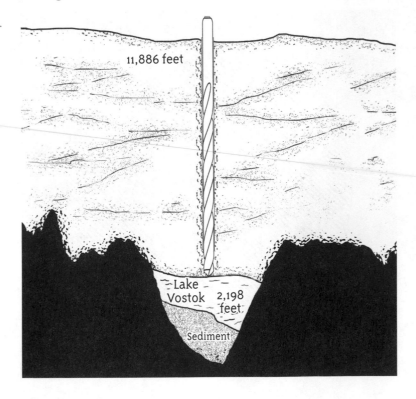

11,886 feet

Lake Vostok 2,198 feet

Sediment

West Antarctica is much smaller than East Antarctica. But even though it is smaller, it has some amazing features. The lowest and highest points on Antarctica are in this region. The lowest point is an area called the Bentley Subglacial Trench. It is 8,325 feet below sea level. It is the lowest point on Earth that is not covered by ocean, although it is covered by ice. The highest point is Mount Vinson, also called Vinson Massif. The mountain is twelve miles long and eight miles wide. It rises to a height of 16,066 feet above sea level. The peak is named after Carl Vinson. He was a US congressman who convinced the US government to support exploration in Antarctica.

Another incredible feature in West Antarctica is Mount Erebus. Mount Erebus is an active volcano. It's hard to believe that there could be a volcano in a place that is so cold and icy, but Mount Erebus is one of the world's largest volcanoes. It stands 12,448 feet high. From time

Mount Erebus

to time it erupts and shoots out volcanic bombs. A lake of molten lava pools up in the inner crater of the volcano.

The Antarctic Peninsula is a piece of land that juts out from West Antarctica toward South America. It looks a bit like the raised trunk of an elephant. It is a very mountainous region, but it is the easiest region of Antarctica to reach. The peninsula is the warmest region on the continent.

Because of this, it is the breeding ground for many penguins, seals, and seabirds. While the peninsula is a quiet and barren area in the winter, in the spring it is noisy and crowded. Plants can even be found growing among the rocks during the summer months.

Volcanoes Under the Ice

Scientists knew that there were forty-seven volcanoes hidden under the ice in West Antarctica. Then, in 2017, scientists from Scotland discovered another ninety-one volcanoes lying over a mile beneath the ice in this region. This could make this area of Antarctica the most volcanic place on the planet. Up until this time, the area around Mount Kilimanjaro in Africa was thought to contain the most volcanoes.

The volcanoes under Antarctica's ice are between 300 feet and 12,600 feet high. Scientists have not been able to figure out if the volcanoes are active or dormant (inactive). But even if they are not active, the heat they give off could melt the ice above them.

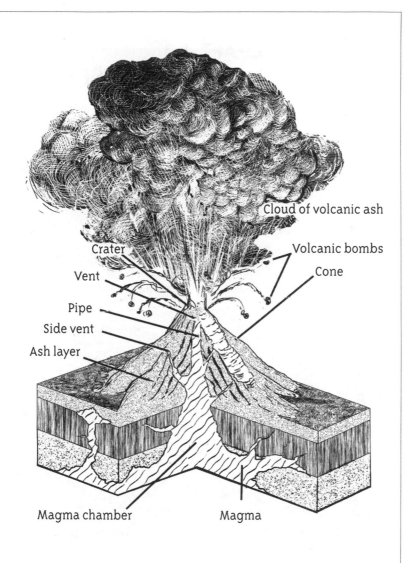

Cloud of volcanic ash

Volcanic bombs

Crater

Cone

Vent

Pipe

Side vent

Ash layer

Magma chamber

Magma

CHAPTER 3
The Coldest Place on Earth

With all the ice on Antarctica, you would think it must snow there a lot. But Antarctica doesn't get much snow at all. In fact, Antarctica is considered a desert. We usually think of deserts as places with miles and miles of sand. But a desert is any region

Sahara Desert in Africa

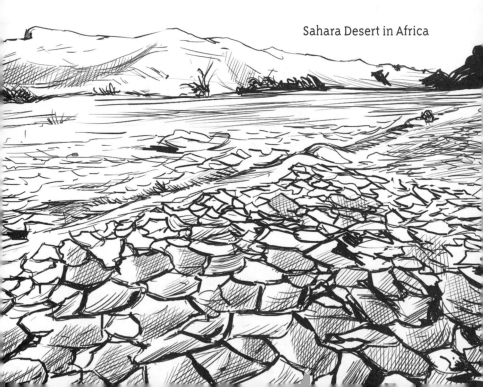

that gets very little precipitation. Precipitation is liquid or solid water that falls from the sky as rain, drizzle, snow, hail, or ice crystals. Antarctica is a desert that is the coldest, driest, and windiest continent on our planet.

You might also think that this frozen continent would have the same climate all over, but that's not so. There are three different climate regions: the interior, the coastal areas, and the Antarctica Peninsula.

The interior of the continent is the coldest and the driest of all the regions. This part of Antarctica gets about the same amount of annual precipitation as Death Valley, California.

Death Valley

Sometimes it is too cold to snow here. Tiny ice crystals known as "diamond dust" fall instead. The average year-round temperature at the center of the continent is –58°F. The coldest

Diamond dust ice crystals

temperature was recorded by Russian scientists in 1983. They recorded a temperature of –129°F! In comparison, the average winter temperature in Chicago that year was 24°F!

This area of Antarctica also experiences fierce winds. The wind can gust up to one hundred miles per hour. As it blows, it picks up drifting snow and causes blizzards that can last for days.

The coastal areas of Antarctica have warmer temperatures and much more snowfall than the interior. The average temperature in the winter ranges from 5° to 15°F, but it can get as cold as –58°F. The region gets a total of twenty to forty inches of snow every year.

This area might be milder than the interior, but it gets even stronger winds. These icy blasts are called katabatic (say: ka-tuh-BA-tik) winds. They start on the high plateaus in the interior and gain strength along the coasts. The highest wind speeds in Antarctica were clocked at 218 miles per hour at Belgrano II station near the Weddell Sea.

The Antarctic Peninsula has the mildest climate on the continent. The average temperature in the summer is above 32°F. The temperature in the winter rarely falls below 14°F. The average precipitation is fourteen to twenty inches a year. Because of the warmer temperatures, it can fall as rain in the summer and snow in the winter.

Emperor penguins

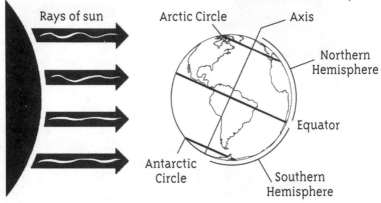

Rays of sun — Arctic Circle — Axis — Summer in the Southern Hemisphere — Northern Hemisphere — Equator — Antarctic Circle — Southern Hemisphere

Some of the differences in the three climates on the continent also have to do with exactly where Antarctica is on our planet. Antarctica is in the Southern Hemisphere. This means that summer lasts from November to March, and winter lasts from April to October. The seasons are the exact opposite of what they are in the Northern Hemisphere. (Also, there is no spring or fall.)

Antarctica is also affected by the way our planet tilts as it turns on its axis. During the summer months, Antarctica is on the side of Earth that is tilted toward the sun. It has constant sunshine during this time. In the winter, Antarctica is on the side of Earth that is tilted away from the sun. The continent has constant darkness during this time.

The nighttime sky above Antarctica puts on a real show. The Milky Way and the planet Jupiter can be seen overhead. The Southern Hemisphere constellations, the Southern Cross and Chamaeleon, cross the nighttime sky at different times of the year.

Aurora borealis

But the greatest light show is the southern lights. Most people have heard of the northern lights (aurora borealis) that appear in the sky in the Northern Hemisphere. But there are also southern lights (aurora australis) in the Southern Hemisphere.

In the north, long ago, people thought these
mysterious displays were signs from the gods. But
we now know that these amazing displays of light
are caused by electrically charged particles that
are given off by the sun. As these particles pass by
our planet, they are attracted to the two magnetic

poles. These particles react with elements in our atmosphere as they get closer. This reaction creates the dazzling lights that can range from orange and green to purple and red.

But the best places to see the southern lights in Antarctica are in some of the hardest places to get to and at the coldest time of the year. So not many people get to witness the spectacular light show there.

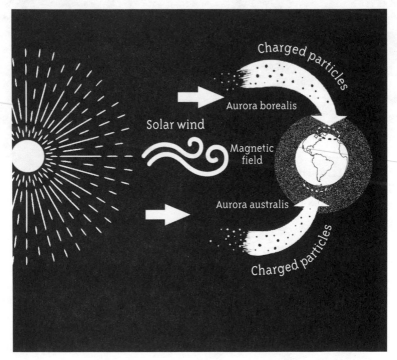

CHAPTER 4
The Unknown Southern Land

Explorers didn't actually see the continent of Antarctica until 1820. But the ancient Greeks believed an unknown land existed somewhere to the south.

In the sixth century BC, Pythagoras (say: peh-THA-guh-rus), a Greek philosopher and mathematician, suggested that Earth was round. In the fourth century BC, another ancient Greek philosopher, Aristotle (say: AHR-iss-tah-tuhl), took this idea even further. He said that if the earth was round, the weight of the land in the

Aristotle

Northern Hemisphere must be balanced by land that lay to the south. Aristotle even gave this land to the south a name. The lands at the top of the planet were under a constellation called Arktos. So Aristotle called the land at the bottom of the planet *Antarktos*, which means "opposite of the north."

Ptolemy (say: TOL-uh-mee), who lived in Alexandria in ancient Egypt, was important in the history of mapmaking. In the second century AD, he put this landmass to the south on a map he made. He called it the "unknown southern land." But Ptolemy thought it was connected to the other continents. He also believed that people lived there and that it had fertile soil.

Centuries passed before anyone tried to prove that this unknown southern land actually existed. In the 1400s and 1500s, European explorers, such as Bartolomeu Dias, Vasco da Gama, and Amerigo Vespucci, began to sail south.

Ptolemy

These explorers were looking for routes to Asia either by sailing around South America or the tip of Africa. They recorded what they saw and shared the information with the rest of the world. But none of them got close enough to this landmass to the south to prove that it was really there.

In 1520, during a voyage around the whole planet, Portuguese explorer Ferdinand Magellan sailed around the tip of South America through a narrow passage of water, later named the Strait of Magellan. It connects the Atlantic and Pacific Oceans. The sailors spotted land to the south as

they crossed the passage. It turned out to be just one of the islands that lie along the southern tip of South America. Many more explorers followed Magellan's course and discovered many more islands in this area. Still, no one had spotted the unknown southern land.

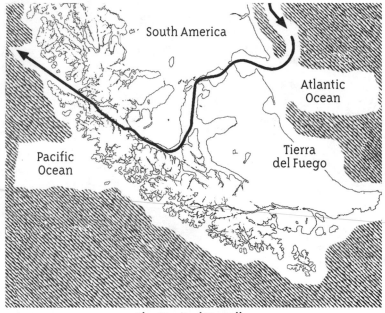

The Strait of Magellan

Did that mean people stopped believing it existed?

Well, some started to doubt.

In 1768, James Cook, a captain in the British navy, was sent to explore the southern Pacific Ocean. As with other explorers before him, the goal was to locate the mysterious landmass. However, Cook returned to England in 1771 without success. He said, "As to a

James Cook

Southern Continent, I do not believe any such thing exists, unless in a high latitude."

Did that mean Cook gave up trying to find what he no longer fully believed in?

No. He was determined to figure out once and for all whether or not *Terra Australis Incognita* existed. (That means Unknown Land of the South.)

In 1773, Captain Cook set off again. There were two ships in the expedition, *Resolution*

and *Adventure*. The crew had enough supplies
for eighteen months and the most up-to-date

chronometer, or timepiece. On this journey, Cook and his men sailed farther south than anyone else ever had. Captain Cook did manage to cross the Antarctic Circle for the first time.

Cook and his crew sailed through bad storms and thick fog on this journey. They came across huge icebergs as well. Cook believed that these icebergs must have broken off from some large landmass.

But as for reaching the fabled southern continent, no. Cook never got there. He and his men returned to England in 1775. He reported that even if there *was* land, the seas were so dangerous and the storms so terrible that no one could possibly live there.

What Cook never knew was that he came within about seventy miles of the coast of Antarctica. That's pretty close. Still, it took almost another fifty years before an explorer finally laid eyes on the unknown southern land.

In 1819, Czar Alexander I of Russia chose Fabian Gottlieb von Bellingshausen to lead an expedition. The czar (emperor) wanted to build more trading posts in that part of the world, so off Bellingshausen went on an extended voyage of discovery.

Fabian Gottlieb von Bellingshausen

Bellingshausen was an experienced sailor. He had been a crew member on the first Russian expedition around the world from 1803 to 1806.

Now he set sail with two ships and nearly two hundred crew members.

Latitude and Longitude

The lines you see on a map or globe are called longitude and latitude lines. These imaginary lines help sailors keep track of where they are. Lines of longitude run between the North and South Poles. Lines of latitude run parallel to the equator. The Antarctic Circle is the name for a special line of latitude. Anything south of the Antarctic Circle is in Antarctica, so the Antarctic Circle is the boundary line for this area of the world.

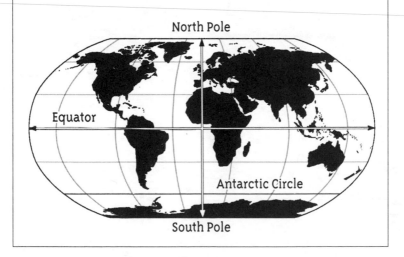

North Pole

Equator

Antarctic Circle

South Pole

On January 26, 1820, the ships crossed the Antarctic Circle. The next day, Bellingshausen and his crew probably made it to within twenty miles of the Antarctic Peninsula. Bellingshausen made a note in his journal that he saw "an icefield with small hillocks." He was the first person who finally laid eyes on Antarctica. But Bellingshausen didn't realize that. Rather than trying to get to the continent, he and his crew sailed on.

Just a year later, Captain John Davis and his crew sailed from Connecticut on a ship called the *Huron*. It was headed to the islands near the Antarctic Peninsula to hunt for seals. When the crew landed, they searched for seals for about an hour, but found none.

On February 7, 1821, the entry in the ship's logbook read, ". . . open cloudy weather and light winds a standing for a large body of land in that direction . . . close in with our boat and sent her on shore . . . I think this southern land to be a continent." Davis and his crew had been hunting for seals, not looking for the unknown southern land. Their discovery opened a new era in exploration.

CHAPTER 5
The Race for the Pole

There was now real proof that a continent existed at the bottom of the earth. That spurred on new groups of explorers. They wanted to discover more of this new continent. They each wanted to lay claim to these lands for their country in hopes that there would be gems and minerals to mine and animals that would provide furs and skins.

James Weddell led a mission to Antarctica from 1822 to 1824. He had been an officer in the British navy, but left to sail commercial ships that hunted seals. In 1823, Weddell sailed down the eastern coast of the

James Weddell

Antarctic Peninsula. He discovered a large body of water, which he called the George IV Sea after the British king at that time. It was later named the Weddell Sea. Weddell also discovered a new type of seal, which was named after him.

When Weddell returned to England, he wrote a book about his journey called *A Voyage Towards the South Pole*. People were fascinated by what he and his crew had seen.

From 1838 to 1840, Charles Wilkes led the first official US expedition to Antarctica. The crew included seven scientists. They went along to study and record the animals, plants, rocks, and minerals that they found. The team also included two artists. They painted and drew the

amazing landscapes they saw along the way. (This was before photography was invented.) Wilkes and his crew mapped more than 1,500 miles of Antarctica's coastline.

British navy captain James Ross and his crew of 134 men set sail in 1839. Eight years earlier he had located the magnetic North Pole. Now he wanted to find the magnetic South Pole. Although he and his crew did not locate the pole, they went farther south than Weddell had. Ross discovered and named Mount Erebus and the large ice shelf that was later named after him. He and his men eventually had to turn back because of the thick pack ice—sea ice that is packed together and moves across the ocean. But when he returned to England, Ross was knighted for his brave adventure.

These and many other missions were made to Antarctica in the nineteenth century. But the first two decades of the 1900s are often called the "heroic age" of Antarctic exploration. Fifteen

Geographic versus Magnetic

The geographic South Pole is determined by Earth's spin. It's a spot in the Southern Hemisphere through which Earth's axis passes. The magnetic South Pole is the spot S on a compass toward which a compass needle points. The geographic and magnetic poles are more than 1,600 miles away from each other! And the magnetic pole moves six to nine miles each year. It is moving northwest toward Australia. Because of this movement, the North and South magnetic poles swap places every five hundred thousand years.

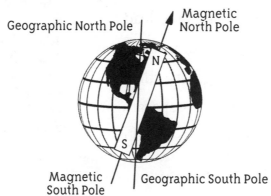

Geographic North Pole

Magnetic North Pole

Magnetic South Pole

Geographic South Pole

expeditions set out to Antarctica during this period. There was a heated race to see who would be first to reach the South Pole.

Robert Falcon Scott had joined the British navy as a cadet at the age of thirteen. In July 1900, at the age of thirty-two, he was named the leader of the British National Antarctic Expedition.

Scott did not have any experience sailing into this part of the world. Nor was he known as a great leader. Many people were surprised he had been given this job. After a year of preparation, Scott and his crew set sail on the *Discovery*.

The ship had been specially built for the journey. It was a sailing ship that also had engines. It also had a bow clad with iron, which was supposed to help the ship cut through the thick ice. *Discovery* was the first ship designed and built in Britain for scientific exploration.

The *Discovery* reached the coast of Antarctica in January 1902. For the next several months, Scott and his crew collected rock and plant samples. They also mapped the area around them. Scott even went up in a balloon.

In November, Scott and two of his crew, Ernest Shackleton and Edward Wilson, began the long journey to the South Pole. They had five sleds pulled by nineteen dogs. They traveled for two months through persistent fog. The ice was slippery and full of deep cracks. The winds were harsh and often blew up so much snow that the men couldn't see where they were going. They were exhausted and had not brought enough food. When they were 480 miles away from the geographic South Pole, Scott realized that there was no way they would make it there and then back to the ship. He decided that they had to turn back. Scott's inexperience meant the expedition ended in failure.

Ernest Shackleton (second from the left)
with his crew from the *Nimrod*

In 1907, Ernest Shackleton led his own British expedition to Antarctica. He and his crew, along with dogs and ponies to pull sleds, set sail on the *Nimrod*. The expedition reached Antarctica in January 1908. In October, Shackleton and three of his men left their camp and started for the

South Pole. Like Scott, Shackleton and his team were not prepared for the tough trek. Although they made it farther than Scott had—they got within ninety-seven miles of the geographic South Pole—they were forced to turn back before reaching their goal.

Roald Amundsen was an experienced Norwegian explorer. Originally he had his sights set on reaching the North Pole. But when he heard that others had beaten him there, Amundsen turned his focus on the South Pole. He was bent on doing what no one had quite yet done.

Amundsen and his crew reached the coast of Antarctica in the fall of 1911. Amundsen was much better prepared for the treacherous journey than the expeditions before him. He had brought the right type of clothing, plenty of supplies, and hearty sled dogs. Amundsen also landed his ship, the *Fram*, in a spot that shortened the distance of the trek to the South Pole.

Dressed for Success

Roald Amundsen had spent time in the Arctic. While there, he noticed the type of clothing the native people wore. It was made from reindeer and seal skins. On the expedition to Antarctica, Amundsen issued each member of his crew clothing made from animal skins and furs. It kept them warm and dry.

On Scott's expeditions, the men wore clothing made from wool. They had to wear many layers to keep them warm. These layers were bulky and made it hard to move. And when the wool became wet from blowing snow and sweat, the wool clothing froze stiff.

At the very same time, Robert Falcon Scott was making his second journey to the South Pole. He knew about Roald Amundsen. And more than anything he wanted to beat him. He wanted to plant a British flag in the ice at the South Pole before Amundsen was able to place a Norwegian flag there. It truly was a race to the pole.

On January 4, 1911, Scott's ship, the *Terra Nova*, reached Antarctica. Scott and his team spent the next several months building supply huts along the route they would take to the South Pole.

On November 1, sixteen men, ten ponies, and thirty-three dogs set out for the pole. After trudging almost eight hundred miles in freezing temperatures across dangerous ice, Scott reached the South Pole on January 17, 1912 . . . only to find a Norwegian flag flying and a tent beside it!

Inside the tent was a note from Amundsen dated December 16, 1911. The note read "Dear

Captain Scott, As you probably are the first to reach this area after us, I will ask you kindly to forward this letter to King Haakon VII. If you can use any of the articles left in the tent please do not hesitate to do so. With kind regards I wish you a safe return. Yours truly, Roald Amundsen."

Scott and his men couldn't believe it!

Amundsen and his team had beaten them to the South Pole by thirty-four days.

Scott wrote in his ship log "Well, we have turned our back now on the goal of our ambition with sore feelings . . . Good-bye to most of the day dreams."

Left Behind

Amundsen and his men named their tent at the South Pole *Polheim* or "Home at the Pole." The tent remains where it was erected, buried beneath the snow and ice. Over the years, many historians and scientists felt it was important to dig it out and put it in a museum. But in 2005, it was decided to leave the tent at the South Pole exactly where it is. It has been declared a cultural heritage site and will continue its chilly journey to even greater depths below the ice.

The hut that Scott used on his first Antarctic expedition still stands. It has become a museum. It serves as a reminder that the exploration of this frozen continent was difficult and treacherous. And the exploration of this continent at the bottom of the world continues to this day.

The Terra Nova hut was Scott's home
during his first Antarctic expedition.

The team of British men struggled to get back to their camp. On the return, they were hit by more severe weather. Scott and his four team members all died. Eight months later, the men's frozen bodies were found along with their tent.

Ernest Shackleton was also disappointed when he heard the news about Roald Amundsen's achievement. He, too, had wanted to be the first person to reach the South Pole. Shackleton made two more trips to Antarctica in his life. In 1914, he planned to walk across the entire continent. It was a bold and brave idea—and almost ended in disaster. As Shackleton and his men prepared for the trek, their boat, the *Endurance*, was crushed by ice. He and his crew fought to survive. It took them almost a year and a half to make it back home. Still, they were lucky to have survived.

Shackleton's final expedition to the South Pole left England in 1921. He hoped to sail around Antarctica. However, Shackleton became sick

on this journey and he died on his way south.
Shackleton's death brought the heroic era of
Antarctic exploration to a close.

CHAPTER 6
Amazing Animals

Survival in Antarctica's climate is difficult, as so many explorers learned. Plants and animals must endure freezing temperatures and months of darkness. But despite these harsh conditions, the environment is home to lots of creatures that swim, fly, and waddle.

Frozen Fish

Why don't fish freeze in the cold water around Antarctica? This question puzzled researchers for many years. We now know that fish in this frozen climate have special proteins in their blood. The proteins act like an antifreeze. They are more powerful and work better than any antifreeze that people use in their cars. The proteins stop the water in a fish's blood from freezing and turning it into a "fish-cicle."

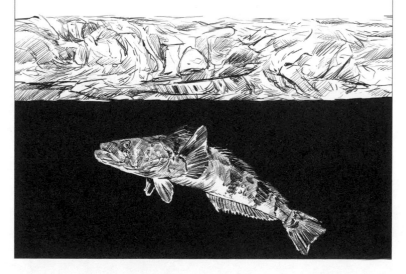

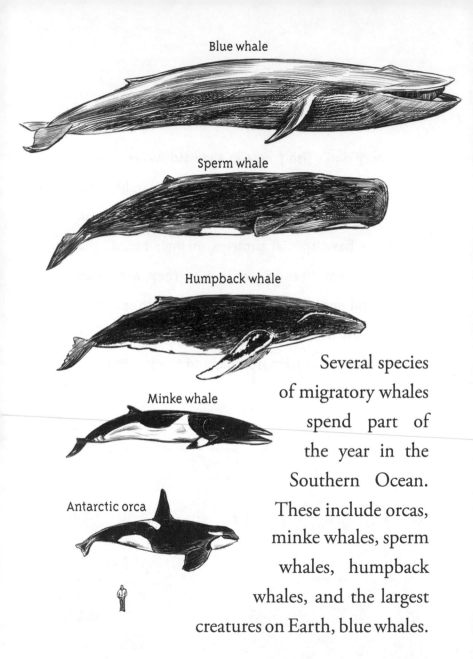

Blue whale

Sperm whale

Humpback whale

Minke whale

Antarctic orca

Several species of migratory whales spend part of the year in the Southern Ocean. These include orcas, minke whales, sperm whales, humpback whales, and the largest creatures on Earth, blue whales.

A blue whale may grow to one hundred feet long and weigh more than 200 tons (400,000 pounds). But this giant creature feeds on one of the smallest creatures that live in this part of the world—the Antarctic krill. The krill is a shrimp-like creature that is only a little over two inches long. The blue whale can take in 15,000 gallons of water—and all the krill swimming in it—in one gulp. A blue whale can eat almost five tons of krill in one day.

The whales in this environment are visitors. They head north to warmer waters when winter arrives. Six different species of seals, however, live there all year round. They have adapted to the extreme weather in this part of the world. Their thick layers of blubber and dense fur keep them warm. The smallest is the fur seal. A female fur seal weighs only about 165 pounds. But a male elephant seal may weigh up to 8,800 pounds. The Weddell seal, named after explorer James Weddell, lives farther south than any other animal. Weddell seals can dive to a depth

Fur seal

Southern male elephant seal

of two thousand feet and can stay underwater for almost an hour as they hunt for fish and squid.

The leopard seal is named for its spotted fur. Its coat resembles the coat of leopards that live in Africa and Asia. Leopard seals are fierce predators. They use their powerful jaws and sharp teeth to hunt fish, penguins, and even other seals.

The sky above Antarctica is home to many types of seabirds, including skuas, petrels, terns, gulls, and albatrosses. Seabirds are

Skua

birds that spend most of their time around the water and get most of their food from the sea. Most seabirds only spend time on land to breed and hatch their eggs. Each spring, over one hundred million birds come to the coast of Antarctica to breed. For the rest of the year, these birds fly over the ocean searching for food.

One of these seabirds is the wandering albatross. It has the largest wingspan of any bird in the world— more than eleven feet

Antarctic petrel

Terns

from tip to tip! A wandering albatross may stay at sea for up to a month in search of food. Its large wings help it glide on the air currents over the ocean. A wandering albatross can cover more than six thousand miles during this time. When a wandering albatross chick leaves the nest, it may not return to land for five to seven years. And

Albatross

when it does finally return, it goes to the exact same island where it was hatched and raised.

Scientists wondered how these seabirds could fly for such long periods without sleep. But it has recently been proven that many seabirds actually sleep while flying. They are able to do this by "shutting down" and resting one half of their brain at a time. But these birds still only get about forty minutes of sleep every twelve hours.

Southern rockhopper

Macaroni

Probably the most famous animals that live in Antarctica are the penguins. There are more than fifteen kinds of penguins that live in this part of the world. Although penguins are birds, they cannot fly. Instead, they are expert swimmers. The types of penguins in Antarctica include the rockhopper, macaroni, Adélie, chinstrap, and the emperor penguin.

Adélie   Chinstrap   Emperor

Emperor penguins

Emperor penguins are the biggest penguins in the world. They can grow to be up to four feet tall. This is the only penguin species that breeds during the winter. Once the female has laid an egg, the male looks after and hatches it. When the egg hatches, the male keeps the chick warm by resting it on his feet.

During blizzards, emperor penguins may huddle in groups of up to five thousand. They take turns moving from the outside to the inside where it is warmest.

Salt-Free!

When seabirds spend so much time at sea, there is no fresh water for them to drink. How do they survive with just salt water to drink? The salt that the birds take in is absorbed into their bloodstream. The salt moves through their blood to a pair of glands just above their eyes. The glands help remove the salt from their system. This salty fluid is excreted, or passed out, through the bird's nostrils and runs down grooves in its bill. If you see a seabird shaking its head, it is probably because it is shaking off drops of this salty liquid from the end of its beak.

From some of the tiniest to the largest creatures on the planet, the isolated and frozen world of Antarctica is home to some of the most fascinating animals on Earth. And they are one of the reasons why people continue to make their way to this continent at the bottom of the world.

CHAPTER 7
More to Explore

The "heroic age" of Antarctic exploration ended in the early 1900s. But since that time, people have continued to travel to Antarctica on adventurous expeditions. Scientists also travel there to learn more about the continent and our planet.

About thirty-two countries operate research stations in Antarctica. There are more than forty permanent stations on the continent. During the summer, there are about four thousand people at these stations. But that number drops to around one thousand in the winter months. The US operates three of the permanent research stations in Antarctica.

One is McMurdo Station. It was named for

Archibald McMurdo. He traveled to Antarctica with Captain James Ross. The US opened this base in 1956.

McMurdo Station

McMurdo Station sits on a patch of black volcanic rock near the Ross Ice Shelf and Mount Erebus. The station is known as "Mac-Town," and it is like a small city. There are about one hundred buildings at the site. Telephone, power, water, and sewer lines zigzag across the station. There are three airfields, a firehouse, a power plant, lots of warehouses and dormitories, and of course lots of research labs. There is also a barbershop, a post office, and a gym.

A few times a week, cargo planes drop off people and supplies. The planes leave with samples from scientific experiments. They also take away garbage and waste material.

McMurdo Station is operated by the US Antarctic Program, but scientists from all over the world live and work there. There are geologists who study rocks and minerals. Meteorologists come to study the weather and climate. Ecologists learn about the environment. Astronomers come to study the stars, planets, and objects in space. Glaciologists are there to study snow and ice— and there is a lot of it to study.

Every February or early March, the last plane flight leaves McMurdo Station. Just over one hundred people stay at the station for the winter. They keep the station running until it reopens in the summer. The workers who remain must withstand months of fierce winds, freezing temperatures, and complete darkness.

In 1957, scientists from around the world organized the International Geophysical Year (IGY). The purpose was for scientists to study the earth and share their findings. More than ten thousand scientists from sixty-seven countries participated. Around the world, about 2,500 IGY stations were set up. More than fifty of them were located on Antarctica. Researchers from twelve countries—Argentina, Australia, Belgium, Chile, France, Japan, New Zealand, Norway, Russia, South Africa, the United Kingdom, and the US— spent time researching everything from volcanoes and glaciers, to plant life on Antarctica.

Antarctic Adventures

Explorers and adventurers continue to travel to the unknown southern land to try to break or set new records. Here are some of the most recent and unusual:

1989–1990—American Will Steger led the first dogsled crossing of Antarctica. The journey took seven months and the team traveled over 3,700 miles.

1994—Liv Arnesen of Norway became the first woman to ski solo in Antarctica all the way to the South Pole.

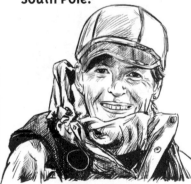

Liv Arnesen

2012—Felicity Aston from England became the first person to ski solo across Antarctica, as well as the first woman to cross Antarctica alone.

2014—At the age of sixteen, Lewis Clarke from England became the youngest person to reach the South Pole.

2014—American Daniel Burton became the first person to ride a bicycle from the coast of Antarctica to the South Pole.

2017—Mike Horn from Switzerland completed the longest unsupported solo crossing of Antarctica. He traveled a distance of just over 3,100 miles using skis and kites.

Mike Horn

The IGY made people recognize how important Antarctica is to the planet and how important it is to preserve it. In 1959, the twelve countries that had set up stations in Antarctica created the Antarctic Treaty. No country owns Antarctica and it is governed by rules set out in this treaty.

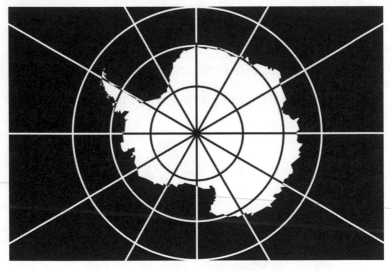

Flag of the Antarctic Treaty

The guidelines state that Antarctica will only be used for peaceful purposes, such as research, exploration, and tourism. Any information that scientists learn from their studies must be shared.

No military forces will be allowed on Antarctica. And nuclear weapons will be prohibited on the continent.

In October 2015, Iceland became the fifty-third country to sign the Antarctic Treaty. Scientists, researchers, and politicians around the world continue to recognize the importance of preserving this unique and special place on our planet.

Women in Antarctica

For many years, women were not allowed to travel to Antarctica. In 1935, Norwegian Caroline Mikkelsen was the first woman to visit the continent. She had traveled there with her husband, who was the captain of a whaling ship. However, when the US opened McMurdo Station in 1956, women were not even

Caroline Mikkelsen

permitted on the ships that traveled there. It was thought that women weren't physically or mentally strong enough to withstand the harsh climate.

In 1969, the US Navy lifted the ban against American women working in Antarctica. Four women from Ohio State University were the first team chosen to travel there. That same year, Dr. Christine Müller-Schwarze arrived. She was the first woman to do scientific research on the Antarctic mainland.

Today, about a third of the people working and doing research on Antarctica are women.

CHAPTER 8
Antarctica Today

Traveling to Antarctica today is very different from the days of Captain James Ross, Ernest Shackleton, Robert Scott, and Roald Amundsen. Tourism to the continent began in the late 1960s. But at that time, few visitors wanted to venture to this place at the bottom of the world. With the development of faster planes and boats, tourism began to increase rapidly in the early 1990s.

From 1990 to 1991, about 4,700 tourists visited Antarctica. Just twenty years later, the number of visitors per year had grown to around 38,000.

Tourists travel to Antarctica for adventure and to see one of the world's most unspoiled places. There they can see the amazing wildlife that only lives in this part of the world. They can also see the huge glaciers and icebergs that only exist in this place. Visiting Antarctica truly is an adventure of a lifetime.

When tourism to this continent began, the boats that carried passengers were fairly small. They usually carried fewer than two hundred people. But today, boats that carry up to three thousand passengers travel through the waters around Antarctica. These larger boats and the large number of visitors create environmental challenges.

The pollution from the ship fuel and the garbage and waste from those tourists can easily spoil this clean continent. An oil spill could be disastrous. Tourists going ashore can disturb the landscape and the wildlife. It is a fine balance to let people discover Antarctica without ruining it.

Helping Native Plants and Animals

Roald Amundsen and Robert Falcon Scott brought dogs with them on their expeditions. And Ernest Shackleton brought ponies to Antarctica to help on his treks across the continent. But scientists later realized that these "nonnative species" could cause harm to the environment. They could bring germs and diseases that might destroy this special ecosystem. So in the 1980s, the Environmental Protocol was put in place. It was created to

conserve the plants and animals that were native to Antarctica. All nonnative species, except humans, had to be removed from Antarctica. And all dogs had to be removed from the continent by 1994.

Even though nonnative species are no longer allowed on Antarctica, scientists and tourists who travel there must be careful. They must be sure not to bring insects, seeds, or small organisms on their clothes, shoes, luggage, or gear. Paying close attention to what enters this environment means that it will be preserved for travelers in the future.

However, it isn't just tourism that threatens the continent. This spectacular environment is also under threat from climate change. The earth is warming up. This is due to an increase in the amount of carbon dioxide and other "greenhouse gases" in the atmosphere. These gases are mostly created by the fuel that we use to run our cars and heat and cool our homes. And as our planet gets warmer, it affects Antarctica.

Over the past fifty years, the average temperature of the air at the Antarctic Peninsula has risen by five or six degrees Fahrenheit. That might not sound like a big change, but it is. Even a small rise in temperatures can cause big changes. Higher temperatures mean that the ice on Antarctica is melting. When ice melts, it causes the level of the sea to rise. Higher temperatures also cause calving of the glaciers. *Calving* is when large parts of glaciers break off. And a warmer climate also causes changes to plants and animals. They may have trouble reproducing.

Immense Icebergs

Icebergs are formed when large chunks of ice calve, or break off, from the edge of a glacier. This is normal. But in the past few decades, some very large icebergs have been created. Scientists believe this is due to global warming.

In 1995, a large iceberg was formed when an area of the Larsen A ice shelf collapsed. In 2002, the Larsen B ice shelf collapsed and created an even bigger iceberg. Both of these ice shelves are on the Antarctic Peninsula.

Then, in July 2017, a huge part of the Larsen C ice shelf, also on the Antarctic Peninsula, calved from a glacier. This iceberg weighed over a trillion tons and was the size of the state of Delaware. It was the biggest iceberg ever.

Iceberg

Larsen C
ice shelf

These big icebergs pose threats. They are dangerous to ships and boats sailing near the continent. And as the iceberg begins to melt, it will cause the sea level to rise.

Since the first person set foot on Antarctica in 1821, we have learned so much about this magnificent and special place on Earth. There is still so much to learn and there is so much that it can tell us about our planet. However, we must all do our part to help preserve its natural beauty.

Timeline of Antarctica

mya = million years ago

c. 35 mya	Earth begins cooling down, ice sheets appear on Antarctica
1520	Ferdinand Magellan sails through the strait at the tip of South America
1773	Captain James Cook crosses the Antarctic Circle
1820	Captain Fabian Gottlieb von Bellingshausen and his crew are the first to see the "unknown southern land"
1821	Seal hunter Captain John Davis is the first to reach Antarctica
1901–1904	Captain Robert Scott leads an unsuccessful British expedition to reach the South Pole
1909	Ernest Shackleton and three of his crew reach farther south than anyone has traveled on the continent
1911	Roald Amundsen and four of his crew become the first men to reach the South Pole
1935	Caroline Mikkelsen is the first woman to set foot on Antarctica
1956	The United States opens McMurdo Station
1957–1958	The International Geophysical Year (IGY) triggers scientific research on the continent
1959	The Antarctic Treaty is established
1986	The first dinosaur fossil is found on Antarctica
2017	A gigantic iceberg from the Larsen C ice shelf breaks off

Timeline of the World

c. 65 mya	Dinosaurs become extinct
c. 200,000 ya	Modern humans—*Homo sapiens*—begin to evolve
c. 11,600 ya	The last Ice Age ends
c. 27 BC	Start of the ancient Roman Empire when Octavian is declared emperor
AD 1492	Christopher Columbus sails to the New World
1620	Pilgrims sail from England to North America on the *Mayflower*
1687	Sir Isaac Newton sets forth the law of gravity
1776	The American Revolution begins
1861	Start of the US Civil War
1879	Thomas Edison invents the first practical lightbulb
1917	The United States enters World War I
1920	The Nineteenth Amendment to the US Constitution is ratified, giving women the right to vote
1952	Jonas Salk invents the polio vaccine
1969	Neil Armstrong becomes the first person to walk on the moon
1997	J. K. Rowling's *Harry Potter and the Philosopher's Stone* is published
2008	Barack Obama is elected president of the United States
2017	Hurricanes Harvey, Irma, and Maria strike the Caribbean and United States

Bibliography

*Books for young readers

Averbuck, Alexis, and Cathy Brown. *Antarctica.* Melbourne, Australia: Lonely Planet Publications, 2012.

*Buckley, James, Jr. *Who Was Ernest Shackleton?* New York: Penguin Workshop, 2013.

Day, David. *Antarctica: A Biography.* New York: Oxford University Press, 2013.

*Friedman, Mel. *Antarctica.* New York: Children's Press, 2009.

*Hirsch, Rebecca. *Antarctica.* New York: Children's Press, 2013.

McGonigal, David. *Antarctica: Secrets of the Southern Continent.* Buffalo, NY: Firefly Books, 2008.

*Petersen, Christine. *Learning about Antarctica.* Minneapolis: Lerner Publishing Group, 2015.

Walker, Gabrielle. *Antarctica: An Intimate Portrait of a Mysterious Continent.* Boston: Houghton Mifflin Harcourt Publishing Company, 2013.

Websites

www.coolantarctica.com

www.livescience.com/21677-antarctica-facts.html

www.nasa.gov/audience/forstudents/k-4/stories/nasa-knows/ what-is-antarctica-k4.html